Kharis A. Reedus

DE LUNA: THE LIGHT IN MY DARKNESS

AUSTIN MACAULEY PUBLISHERS™

LONDON • CAMBRIDGE • NEW YORK • SHARJAH

Ordering Information
Quantity sales: Special discounts are available on quantity purchases by corporations, associations, and others. For details, contact the publisher at the address below.

Publisher's Cataloging-in-Publication data
Reedus, Kharis A.
de Luna: The Light in My Darkness

ISBN 9781647509613 (Paperback)
ISBN 9781647509620 (Hardback)
ISBN 9781647509637 (ePub e-book)

Library of Congress Control Number: 2021915013

www.austinmacauley.com/us

First Published (2021)
Austin Macauley Publishers LLC
40 Wall Street, 33rd Floor, Suite 3302
New York, NY 10005
USA

mail-usa@austinmacauley.com
+1 (646) 5125767

To Mom. You are the strongest source of light.

To Papa. You are the closest thing to God I have ever experienced.

To Noni. Your strength amazes me.

Moon

m̄oon/

noun

noun: Moon; noun: moon

the natural satellite of the earth, visible (chiefly at night) by reflected light from the sun.

synonyms: satellite

"an eclipse of the moon"

"And if you are to love,
Love as the moon loves;
It does not steal the night—
It only unveils the beauty of the dark"

ISRA AL-THIBEH

PHREE THE ART
DECAPITATE IT

**To Those Who Are Searching for More Life.
May We Never Be Satisfied.**

Pluto | Purpose | Power
Uranus | Understanding
Neptune | Nostalgia
Saturn | Satisfaction
Mars | Mastery
Earth | Euphoria

Preface

How much time does it take to live a life?
How much pain does it take to learn how to endure?
Is there strength in the phrase "keep going?"
Is there a transition without a shift?
At the beginning of the journey
There is an illusion.
You believed that you learned enough to remain close to
what's familiar
Overlooking the lesson that's trapped inside seclusion.
I have basked in the sun,
I have run in the rain,
I have felt great amounts of pleasure,
And I have had my fair share of shame.
I have seen the unapologetic ocean waves,
I have seen the clouds and the dirtiest water drains,
I have seen the happiest moments of life,
And I have seen the darkness engulf us all the same.
Out of all the life,
I believe I have lived,
There may be only one result.
Honestly, my safest bet

Out of all this time
I have not seen anything yet.

Pluto

Power

Power

"She
In the Dark
Found Light Brighter Than Many Will Ever See.
She
Within Herself
Found Loveliness
Through the Soul's Own Mastery.
And Now
The World Receives
From Her Dower:
The message of the strength
Of inner power."

-Langston Hughes

Power

Political or national strength.
Great or marked ability to do or act
Strength
Might
Force.
Force
Might
Strength
Force
Is
A
Might
That's
Full
Of
Strength
Power
Is
A
Strength
I
Might

Have
To
Force.

Un

How much can I ask for?
How much would you give me?
Would you love for my frequency to become my enemy?
What fuels your fire?
Is it control?
Is it the blueprint to my defeat?
I allowed myself to grow
And harnessed my ankles
I saw no feet.
I saw no forward.
I saw no back.
I saw no gain.
I saw no lack.

Is all power limited?

Deux

The time.
Can you tell me the time?
If I cannot tell you, I know it's not mine.

I own nothing.

Trois

You disappeared into a reflection,
Uncertain of the destination,
You made me chase my shadow,
Because it represented the darkness you remained in
So—
I believe I could find you in a place where even the
boisterous are attentive,
Or maybe, if I dropped my chord, you'd be below an
octave—
I painted a picture with your smile today.

I don't have the strength to find you.

Quatre

You See, the Sea Doesn't Ask for Air
It Just Breathes.
You Grab Too Much.
You Waste Too Little.
You Secure Yourself in a Foundation Too Brittle.
You Don't Want Anything to Do With Yourself.
Control it.

Love Yourself More, Please.

Cinq

Love Will Be Wherever You Plant it.
Control Yourself.

Six

What breaks?
Force.
What heals?
Time.

Sept

You've Never Met Your Strength.
You're Aware of What Bothers You,
You Comfort What Scares You,
You See What Makes You Blind,
You Sit When You're Tired,
But You Don't Know Your Strength.
You've Embraced Your Worries,
You've Apologized to Your Wounds,
You've Fallen on a Ground Your Feet Never Touched,
You Found the Perfect Way to Distract Yourself,
But You Never Found Your Strength.
You Had No Choice But to Continue to Live,
But You Never Found Your Strength.

Did You Even Notice?

Huit

There is Power in Peace and Placement.
The Power of Love Has Been Planted,
With a Seed-
In a Pot-
That Has Been Banished.
You Ever Tried to Build a Home You Couldn't Manage?
Me, You see,
I am a Soul,
You Could Never Meet
Is it There?
Could Be…
Your Power Is There.
Believe me.
It's Not a Piece of Clothing You Can Wear.
You Can't Make People Stop and Stare.
Your Soul Is a Garnet Made in Heaven with the Strength
to Destroy a Pair
Have You Found Your Placement?

Where Is Your Place?

Neuf

Phree the Power
Don't Hold it Down
Phree the Power
Rob it From the Clowns.

Dix

Clashing
Gnashing
Clashing
Gnashing.
The Sound of Confliction
Is Clashing
&
Gnashing.

Onze

I Won't Apologize Anymore,
I Won't Apologize for My Head Held High,
You See,
I Wasn't Always This
Brave.
I Hid My Spirit in Something Like a Cave,
Resulted in a Plan to Raise a Hardened Spirit with a Blind
Brigade.
I Wanted a Leader.

I Didn't Know I Was Lost.

Douze

I Look into the Sky,
Such A Reality.
The Aurora of the Light Reminds Me.
Of Who I Could Be,
If I Let Me.

Treize

27

The Fifth Hour Gave Me the Insight That Something Was
Wrong.
A Day Isn't Supposed to Last This Long.
How Much Can I Give You for a Night?
Not Intimacy
But a Chance to Run from Daylight
You Expose Me
You Remind Me of So Much I've Tried to Forget About.

No Hiding Place.

Quatorze

I Turn on the TV and See Them.
Trapped.
I Walk Away.
And I Release Them.
Phree.

Fame Is an Illusion.

Quinze

I declare that I have won.
There wasn't a contest,
There wasn't a race,
I got to where I am,
By being in last place.

Persistence.

Seize

Wild Is the Soul That *Isn't* Content
I Forgave My Power
I Forgave My Cowardly Power
I Forgave My Light
I Believed it Not to Exist
Wild Is the Soul That *Missed* its Kiss
Wild Is the Soul with No Patience to Sell
Your Power Is Wherever You Plant it

Control Yourself.

Mindful.

Dix-Sept

Allow Myself to Re-Enter This Room…
I May Have Shut the Door but Please Let Me In
You See I Never Believed That I'd Be Back Again.
Where Can I Shelve My Sanity?
Where Can I Place My Humility?

Should I Rearrange My Sadness?

Should I Toss Out My Reluctance?

I tried to find you again.

Better.

Dix-Huit

I buried my winter today,
To water my summer.

Warmer Nights.

Dix-Neuf

The Peace Within Is the Peace Without
When There Is No Peace Do Not Count Me Out.
With My Peace,
Comes a Hint of Doubt,
With My Peace,
Comes Problem on a Mount,
Within My Peace,
Is a Sense of Power That Exceeds Any Amount,
Never Did I Say My Peace Wasn't Rough,
I've Always Said My Peace Was Just Enough.

Vingt

Patient is the **woman** that has great faith
Love is the **woman** that grows
Harmful is the **woman** that's naive
Powerful is the **woman** who knows.

Vingt-et-Un

I Possess the Power to Free My Release,
Bound Up My Reality and Let My Wild Run Free,
I Take Part in My Own Uplifting,
And Fuel My Own Demise,
Understanding the Freedom Within,
My Power Will Take Time.

Vingt-Deux

I Woke Up.
Powerless.
Unable to Communicate.
Fully Capable of Making Mistakes.
I Woke Up.
Powerful.
Every Word Said.
Meaningful.

Vingt-Trois

There Is Power in the Good Things.

Vingt-Quatre

You See the Tranquility in My Uncertainty
You Held My Head High
You've Placed Joy in My Mouth
When I Only Had the Strength to Cry
With No Reluctance to Acknowledge My Burdens
You Crowned Me Before I Ever Entered My Palace
You Showed Me Love Before I'd Ever Been Hurt
We Will Never Part.
You're Never Far
But There Was No Sight of You
There Was No Hint.
You Were Fully Present
And I Never Caught Your Scent.

Vingt-Cinq

You escaped.
Power, I freed you
I thought being held captive in my presence would
disappoint you
Or rob you of your worth.
I couldn't have you,
I didn't deserve you,
You see, I'm unhappy.
And unhappy people are dangerous.
Life is wherever you plant it.
Control Yourself.

Vingt-Six

The foundation of your power is your strength
You Are Unable to Listen to the Cries
You Are Conflicted Inside—
You Are an Emotional Ocean Tide
There are other ways to sail this ship
There are other ways to rise.
You strip the wealth
You've robbed the youth
You're deaf to the purpose
And you pacified me with a portion of the truth
You removed every single part of me
Confidence
Confusion
Happiness
Sadness
Hope
Faith
Fear
You robbed me of all my strength
You robbed me
You Robbed Me of All I've Known in This Life
Until power was the only thing I had left.

Vingt-Sept

Power, you're blind.

Vingt-Huit

I painted a picture of a conqueror
I almost forgot how I looked.

Vingt-Neuf

43

I could've given so much,
And received so little,
The cost of loss from a giving heart,
Left my foundation so brittle.

Trente

Now that I have you where I want you,
I want you to be still.
I want you to choreograph every step my heart takes,
I want my life to be your will.
Now that I have you where I want you,
I want you to remain,
I want you to water me,
While you stay the same.

Power, I Found You.

URANUS

UNDERSTANDING

Understanding
"Peace cannot be
Kept by force;
It can only be achieved
By understanding."

– Albert Einstein

un ·der ·stand ·ing

[uhn-der- **stan**-ding]

NOUN

1.

mental process of a person who comprehends; comprehension; personal interpretation: *My understanding of the word does not agree with yours.*

2.

intellectual faculties; intelligence; mind: *a quick understanding.*

3.

superior power of discernment; enlightened intelligence: *With her keen understanding she should have become a leader.*

4.

knowledge of or familiarity with a particular thing; skill in dealing with or handling something: *an understanding of accounting practice.*

5.

a state of cooperative or mutually tolerant relations between people: *To him, understanding and goodwill were the supreme virtues.*

I had to force myself to make room for my understanding.
I valued knowing exactly how, when, and why I did what I
did.
To be clear and concise in my decisions, heartfelt in my
answers.
To understand myself is to be confident in my ability to
sustain a healthy outlook on my well-being, all while
nurturing the parts of myself that aren't yet to be
uncovered.
To understand myself is to maintain a sense of security in
myself in the midst of all the chaos life brings.
To understand myself is to dive deeper into my pain, my
anguish, and my disappointment.
To understand myself is to be the only source of joy I will
ever know.
To understand myself is the beginning of loving myself.

Oil | Water

The night is still young while we converse on a subject
that we call our own
The ceiling baring all of our bad news
The underlying message behind our dying connection
The distance between our two worlds is further than any
other
And we're trying our best to sympathize, empathize, and
realize that we can't understand where we refuse to stand.
You spoke in mountains
Thought in streams
You claimed reality
And I only claimed dreams.
I bled tornadoes
Talked in flames
We lived the same life
But nothing was the same.
I believed in colors
You believed in grey
And both of us couldn't understand
Why the other would live their life this way.

"One"

I walked up to you in such a kind manner
Wondering how you'd react to see a face you've
mistreated
The look of shock caressed your aroma,
But I must admit that you carried yourself well.
How did it feel to lose the idea of something great?
Only time will tell
Leave that tainted oil in the well
Every season is needed to progress or fail
The hardest battles are the ones we remember
December is just as valued as September
There was no need to cry
No need to deprive
As soon as the moon leaves
He makes room for something better to arrive
As I walk away
I look back and realize that I chose to see
What my fantasy wanted to see in my reality
Between the second guessing
The doubt
The time given to a dead situation
The feeling that there's no way out

I ran into the nearest bar
Grabbed a spot on the dance floor
I loved the sound of relief
Hard feeling to ignore
Dropping whiskey all over my zone
The freedom I carried
Left room for more song
Understood that I needed nobody to take me home.

Hopeful

You were red.
Consuming.
Bloody.
Giving life.
Sustaining purpose.
Without me
You left the scene
Human
&
Hopeless.

There isn't much time left for the hopeless.

Excerpt

Understand That You Need to Protect the Fuck Out of
Yourself
Understand That You Need to Hear Your Deepest Cries in
the Beginning
Understand That You Need to Hold Your Own Hand in
the End
Understand That Crying in the Place of Laughter Is the
Result of Healing
Understand That There Are Times When You Won't
Understand
And You Won't Grow.
And You Won't Heal.
And You Won't Know.

Ties

When you suffer, I feel
When you scream, I ache
Darling you believed that we were too far apart to claim
And my soul understood that we were achingly the same.

Heard

The banging of the shadows against your chest
Showed the confidence of a woman who pretended to love
herself
But often saw herself as second best
She knew the path
She easily took a breath
She knew how to stand tall and speak amongst the rest
At night she would capture the stars
Took a trip to Venus
Amazed by the beauty that was called Mars
The thunder roared as she became upset
Her loneliness became a tsunami of doubt
The world went dark
While she screams and shouts
She believed that no one heard the sound of her screams
She was her sun
Every morning she rose to the sky
Drenched in her own ashes
Conqueror of her own time
The power she had wasn't understood by mortals
But the eternal found her sublime
The clouds softened her falls

The trees covered her torture
The moon blushed when she arrived
And she believed no one heard her.

Will you still love me the very second you stop understanding why?

Grasp

The many hands that have touched my soul have left me
tainted
The bronze glow that shines from the bottom of my
electric soul
Shows that there's more
If you never held more
You could never hold me.

Teacher

You taught me how to be
~~Un~~selfish in a world where we bury the selfless
I was afraid that my caring would show
You weren't in danger
Because you couldn't care less.

Who's your sponsor?

Could've

We could've honestly—
We couldn't of done anything honestly
You never believed in the truth
And your reflection lied every time
I understood that nothing was meant to be perfect
You understood that you had to pretend
You overlooked the serenity
And I understood that there's more to the beach than just
sand.

For Once

I
Want
You
To
Understand
That
All
I've
Ever
Seen
Was
The
Worst
of
Them
All
And
For
Once
I
Want
To

See
The
Sunshine
After
The
Rain.

Run Free

God has blessed me with the knowledge of the other side
The other side of it all
The knowledge to know how to properly nurture a tree
And the wisdom to not weep when it falls
The ability to swim with the rebels
And to maintain my solitude within a crowded room with
four walls
My spirit is ambitious
The light of my path is none the vicious
Insight beaming with sunlight
Not lacking a hint of sympathy
With overflowing empathy
Unaware of the degree of passion
That can't be handled with just any mindset
To my realization
My love needn't an invitation
It just arrives
It never bothers to say hi
The greetings become old
And the same stories tend to be told
So if there isn't any room
Or any soil left to plant your tree

If there isn't any room
For your soul to run free
The lack of understanding will prevail
And you will always be you
Without the blessing of running away
Free
With
Me.

Loud

Your noise
Equates to my silence
I begged for you to listen
And you begged for me to be quiet
I hear every word you haven't said
You see every disappointment I have in my head
When you got upset
You weren't your very best
Everyone saw it as a tantrum
I saw it as a man
Who always felt that his kingdom was being sold for a
cheap ransom
I wanted you to know
That through all that noise
I saw a man so uncomfortable
But behind every fit
The world ran away
And thought less and less of this
In my silence
I saw a man
Who was defeated
Angry

And sad.
And nobody cared for him.

                              thought you knew.

You
Already
Knew
What
I
Was
Going
To
Say
And
The
Day
Came
When
You
Didn't
And
I
Decided
Then
There
Was
No
Reason
For
Me

To
Stay.

Invasive

Your city is corrupted
My government invaded
I thought you needed help
As you labeled me invasive.

I can't save you from yourself.

"If only"

You
Could
Find
A
Friend
If
You
Knew
How
To
Be
One.

Overseas

Your thoughts
Shallow as the ocean
I could never
Swim that deep.

Unknown territory
Requires a sacrifice
To walk with you
May risk my life.

I knew
You knew
That to share something new
Is something we both hesitated to do.

The journey
That required me and you
To leave
What was familiar
To embrace something new and peculiar
Had to end abruptly

Because I wanted to stay on land
While your love was overseas.

Safe

In a dangerous world
Full of judgment and hate
Your reflection is the only place
Where you know
You are safe.

Became/Become

I've became
Over and over again
I became another version of myself
Over and over again the same
I've became new
Became old
Became a sense of pride
Became numb
Became ignorant
Became obsessive
Became unkempt
I've become so much
I became just like the rest.

I never let myself win
I allowed myself to be second best
I became like the others
I became like the rest.
I had the power to become more
The power to do what seems fit

As I became more involved in what I want to become
The more I realize this isn't it.

**I've understood more of what's been left behind, more
than what is to come.**

Above

Hear me as I say
The world between us
Has no hearsay.

And

Scattering.
When you take a peek beneath the surface of my
insincerity
There is scattering
The lies fall to the ground
My conscious rushes to retrieve the deceit
To show the ultimate color of my aura
Wouldn't that classify as defeat?

You Are Your Own Truth.

Beyond

The layers of your love are mind-boggling
I considered your hugs earth shattering
I believed that your words were blinding
You ~~were~~ are your own light
I surrounded myself in it like
The way a child smothers its mother, like
The way my soul tells me to take cover
In the midst of danger
I depicted you as just another stranger.
You've changed my perspective
Unbothered my constant rejection
You were higher.
You are higher
The birds in the sky are envious of your desire
I complained.
I found that this cosmic energy you held was strange
I wanted a part
I wanted a view
To become less of me and more of you
To increase this bond
For only love like this
Comes from Above and Beyond.

Will You Be Able to Support When You No Longer Understand?

I try to make sense of it all.

If there is ever a lack of understanding,

Please

Forgive me,

Forgive me,

FORGIVE ME.

Forgive me,

Forgive me,

Forgive me,

Forgive me,

Forgive me.

F
O
R
G
I
V
E
M
E

Forgive me,
Please.

"FORGIVE ME"

A SHORT POEM FOR THE GUILTY.

"Anytime"

There will be a time
When your solitude won't leave you alone
It'll sing you a song of lullabies
Revealing images of what you've called home
I was assuming it was the end
I could never have the decency
To allow you to leave my life
So that your shadow will have room to breathe
I submerge myself with recordings of you
Just wanted to hear your voice
Whether you want to come back
That is nothing less than your choice
But just in case
You find yourself wondering if I'm still true
And if the confidence I have is still mine
I'll always understand the need to come back to what's
familiar
And please just stop by when you have the time.

Still I Wait.

"No Need to Rush"

81

The earth
Rotates slowly
Reminding us
To
Remember
How
To
Take
Our
Time.

"Covenant"

I've agreed
To silence
The noisy
Junky
Messy
Evil
Hint
Of
Jealousy
I
Have
When
You
Leave
Me.

Unaware/Unafraid

I am right here
Taking it step by step
Ready to go with **stride**
I walk in the opposite way
Whispering to my pride,
"Right now you cannot stay,"
I am ready to **conquer**
And I cannot get in my own way.
I may have forgotten to consider it
I pretended not to see the fear
Because if I acknowledged the fear
There's a possibility
I wouldn't be standing right here.
Unafraid.
Living.
Bleeding.
Courage.

I am right here
Ready to flourish
Taking it step by step
Soul ready for soarin'

I cannot remember the pain
But if I had to sum it up
I had the courage to walk into the unknown
Which eventually became the **Sun**.

84

Everything you want is on the other side of fear.

"Shattered"

Your ego
Came
And
Left
And bruised my soul.
Your ego
Came
And
Left
My warm
Heart
Cold.
Your ego
Came
And
Left
The truth started to unfold.
Your ego
Came
And Left,
And I Finally Said No.

Because there is no way your tainted feet can walk on my
streets of gold.

SATURN

SATISFACTION

"The Value of Life Lies Not in the Length of Days, But in the Use We Make of Them. Whether You Find Satisfaction in Life Depends Not on Your Tale of Years, But on Your Will."

– Michel De Montaigne

To the ones that I love,

I am here
For as long as God wants me
I am here
For as long as God needs me
And if you ever become saddened by my departure
And you find opposition in the midst of my transition
Know that I am resting well
Satisfied with what's been given
And not plagued with what I felt I was missing
There is satisfaction in the decision that life will remain
Whether I am around to see
The sun will rise
And the ocean will never cease to be
I am guaranteed that the diamonds will dance
And there will be moments where you will be required to
take a second glance
I know you will have moments of joy
Laughter filled nights
I am certain that you'll be comforted by the stars
And you'll fight against depression with all your might
I am certain that the wolves will howl
And the trains' horns will blow

I am certain that after you hit a piano key
There will always be a note below
Whether I am around to see
Or it was time for me to be called home
Just know that I am satisfied
That God will never leave you alone.

I Trust in the Divine.

"?"

What is the price of satisfaction?
Is it the sacrifice of comfort and certainty
With a side of affirmative action?
Is there a time and a place
Where melancholy backs away to give happiness some
personal space?
Your soul screams scarcity
And your mindset is deemed irate
You proclaim to have a belly full of wisdom
But thoughtlessness is the only item being served on your
plate
What is the price of satisfaction?
Can one refuse such a gift?
What if your satisfaction came
And the memory of it is the only thing you have left?
What is the price of satisfaction?
If ungratefulness is the only song a heart sings,
What is the price of satisfaction
If accompanied by frustrations sting?
What is the price of satisfaction
If that's all we expect life to bring?

Happiness

I chase you every lifetime.

"And every ending."

To the sight of doubt,

My eyes are low.

I've Seen Better Things.

"First place"

This world
Has given birth to strength
Homed kingdoms
And destroyed the upright
It has made the most courageous
Fall down and cower
Torn down mountains
And sent the desert acid showers
You were seen
As important
And needed.
There's nothing
That
Is
That
Isn't
Needed.

The relief is the ability to start again,

I have never been half
I have always been whole
The weight of this planet
Cannot compare to the sight of my soul.

Went to sleep, I'm still whole.
Woke up late, but I'm still whole
Wasn't chosen today, but I'm still whole.
Abandoned but I'm still whole
Cheated on but I'm still whole
Forgotten about but I'm still whole
Woke up alone but I'm still whole
Went to sleep together but I'm still whole.

I was listened to but I'm still whole
I wasn't heard and I'm still whole
Apologies never received but I'm still whole
Standing in the corner unacknowledged but I'm still whole
Forgiven, I'm still whole.
Heartbroken, I'm still whole.
Sitting down as a whole.
Standing here and I'm still whole.
Writing this but I'm still whole.
Reading this but I'm still whole.

I have never been half
I have always been whole
If that is something you can't believe
You should take a look at your own soul.

NEPTUNE

NOSTALGIA

**"I Have a Profound Sense
of Nostalgia for Our Youth
And I Think People Need to Come to Terms with
Things Leaving and Being Gone."**

– Cole Sprouse

Sunrise | Sunset

The beauty of the beginning
Is something I had the pleasure of witnessing
To see the majesty of the person that's standing in front of
me
There couldn't be a reason to look away
The newness made me curious
And the uncertainty made me furious
Every second spent was worth the happy
The days spent laughing loudly
At the assumptions that they made of you and me
You were my friend
You were my safety
You enjoyed keeping the faith alive
And I embraced it hastily.
The beauty of the beginning
Is something I had the pleasure of witnessing
To see the destruction
Of a bond being reduced to just an assumption
I no longer needed to know
The uncertainty made me whole
The days I spent angry at those texts
Made me want to make room for the next

You were my friend
You became a memory
I hid from you
And you couldn't stand me.
You were my friend.
The beauty of the beginning
Had no comparison to the beauty of the end.

Uncertain

Now that it is gone are we certain that it will happen
again?
The smile that was plastered because there's a portion of
our time that we finally believed we've mastered
Are we certain that it'll happen again?
The way the night sky projects the safety of itself in my
brown eyes, convincing me that there's no greater time to
be alive–
Are we certain it'll happen again?
The way the waves roar, covering up for the secrets hidden
beneath the ocean floor
Are we certain that it'll happen again?
The day you stayed until sunrise, and listened to my cries–
You said you'd stay over again, you lied
Are we certain that it'll happen again?
What will happen when there's no longer value at our
table?
What will happen when our friends and family can't make
it–
And we're no longer available?
Treasure every moment
Every breath

Every phone call

Every text

Every argument

Every guest

Every wrong move

Every hug

Every day you walk in peace

Every day you fall out of love

Every "what do you want to do next"

Every "I'll meet you outside"

Every "I don't know what to expect"

Every "I don't think I want to do this anymore"

Every second spent rich

Every moment deemed poor

Every "Hey can you give me a ride"

Every pain staking jab at your pride

Value every place you stand.

Because we aren't certain that it'll happen again.

Ousted

I held you captive in my dreams
I pulled you up by your pants and ripped you by the seams
I chained you against the pavement on the surface of my
conscious
The jailhouse is my head
The trial is held by a jury that can't remain focused
I had nothing to do with this pain
You unleashed a fire within me
The kind that destroyed with a small flame
I sat back and let you attack me
I couldn't take responsibility just yet
It was all your fault
And I accomplished nothing with this mindset.
Silent cries beat against your jail cell
I encaged you in a personal hell you'll never even see
I wanted to picture you suffering without me
The jailhouse was filled with pictures of me + you
I wanted to remind you that you'll never get a chance for
us to be completely through
I tortured you with the idea that every person can't fill in
the shoes of us two
Everywhere you went I made sure I was there

The scent of my well-being, my fingers getting stuck in
your hair
Lunch time was the hardest for you I bet
I always knew you didn't know what to do alone at best
I doubted your ability to move on
I ridiculed you at the thought of it
You can't survive without my love
I know that I screamed and shouted.
I wanted you to drown in my tears
I wanted you to run back to my pride
I didn't care if it took years.
You embraced new opportunities
And I comforted my self-pity + fear,
the sleepless nights,
the hunger strikes,
the code reds,
never left my head.
I was chained to a world that never left my bed
I drowned in my own tears
I reminded myself of the good times
I tortured myself for what seemed like years
I storm to your cell
Furious with short sentence
I demanded to see you in my poorly decorated version of
hell
What I saw was something I couldn't believe
There was dust on your bed
No sheets left for free
Piled food on the floor
Cobwebs surrounding me
I yelled a name in a voice so sincere

In the midst of anger, the doubt, and the fear
The tears, the trials, the barbwire I set up near
All this time spent suffering
And you were never here.

Unfamiliar

A taste of the future
Helped me cope with my past
Everything is nothing new repeated
Going to a place somewhat peculiar slow
To a familiar place, fast.

Destination

Who are you running to?
Who are you running for?

Rebirth

I have been forgotten
Thank God,
I have been forgotten
So I can find myself again
Without painting a memory of who I have been.

You, first

Until I see it that we're happy being apart,
I can no longer be happy being a part.

You should learn to love yourself first.

Everything right

I went everywhere you wanted to go
Sat everywhere you wanted me to be
I lived a life as awful without you
Your life as beautiful without me.

I've spent too much time in an environment filled with
fake contentment
The old me had had enough
+ The new me needed a home.

I need a safe place.

Life lesson

Grab that forgiveness.
Up up & away.

Excerpt

Sometimes I wonder
What would've happened if given another chance.
A chance to relive a train wreck, a backstabbing, a
heartbreak, an apology.
What would've happened if my pride wasn't involved?
What could've happened if you were me and I were you?
What if the sky painted oceans,
and the water winds blew?
What if the day you couldn't apologize for the sunrise,
resulted in the decay of the sunset?
You dismantled the possibility of a new day
Something I suppose you knew how to do best.
What if your pride held you as you fell?
What if heaven's gate burned fury as calm as the gates of
hell?

Mantra

Things Will Get Better.
Things Will Get Better.
Things Will Get Better.
Things Will Get Better.
Things Will Get Better.
Things Will Get Better.
Things Will Get Better.
Things Will Get Better.
Things Will Get Better.
Things Will Get Better.
Things Will Get Better.
Things Will Get Better.
Things Will Get Better.
Things Will Get Better.

I promise.

Simple things

I almost forgot the time spent to make me feel special
wasn't much time spent at all.

Cycle

The sight of life
The sight of it all
Is
Crashing
And
Burning
The beginning of life
Is
A
Sight
Crashing
And
Burning.

December

Winter
Arrived
When what fell
Left us deprived
Winter
Arrived
When we were close to running out of time
Winter
Arrived
When it was time to reclaim what was mine
Winter
Arrived
When I let go of who I thought I'd be
Winter
Arrived
To remind me where my soul belonged
Winter
Arrived
After a year running away
Winter
Arrived
To remind me

That when winter arrived
It was time to leave my worries behind
And
Return
Home.

Secret garden

Life has granted me a garden
A pocketful of lilies
And a tree with roots that have hardened
I have decided to uproot
The weeds and the roses that have thorns
I knew there was beauty in the emptiness
And solace in the torn
The water quenches the thirst of the broken
The sunlight serves as a reminder
That when you're trapped in the dirt
Life has always given bad times a timer
You may become soft
You may feel like a coward
But this garden is here to remind you
You're as beautiful as the smallest flower.

Am I dreaming?

My soul yearned for you
In the heat of the night
My eyes were closed to it all
Yet the meaning shined so bright
Have I ever left you?
Isn't it easy to see?
That the day you left
Was the day I thought I still had me?
Even in another dimension
We still had our division
Our souls continue to wonder
Why ~~did~~ we have to abort our mission?
There could've been.
There always "could've been"
If we didn't "could've been"
We would have our chance
To be stronger within
We would've been
Brilliant
Magnificent
Full of faith and trust
The false world believed in us

I loved you ferociously
Spoke to you kindly
And then I woke up.

Tiptoe

I used to stomp
Through
Life
LOUD
And
LIVELY
I used to stomp
Through
Life
Carrying
Everybody
The
More you live
Life
The more you
Will
Know that
The
Best way
To
Live a joyful
Life

Is
To
Take it slow
Carry yourself
And learn to tiptoe.

Again

The same soil
You used to curate this havoc
Is being used again.
The same soil
That's being used to curate a new life
Is being used again.
Again.
And
Again.
You use the same soil.
Again
And
Again
You try to cure
Your own turmoil
With your old soil.

Ground floor

At this time
There might be a skyscraper
With an amazing view
The type to make you leave your home
And start again, with something, somewhat new.
At this time
You may have forgotten
How much dust and debris
Had to become something worth being seen
The newness became old
But that's the part of the story that goes untold
Because no one knows that often glitter is mistaken for gold
The floors had many demons
The stairs hid away secrets
The very bed you're laying on
Is stained with regret
You must've forgotten
That the day you decided to build
You pretended to be confident
While your love and caring spirit decided to take yield
You must've forgotten

There was a time you wanted more
But never forget
That you started on the ground floor.

Unresponsive

One day I begged you to be quiet.
I wanted you to stay away.
You wanted my sunshine.
But I demanded a cloudy day.
One day I begged you to be quiet.
And you didn't listen to a sound I made.
I begged you to be quiet.
And you continued to talk about your day.
How can I forgive myself for being so gray?
I never knew there would be a time
Where you won't be able to talk about your day.
Time has gone by
And now I have time to be attentive.
Unfortunately, that was the day
You were deemed unresponsive.

Unappreciated

The unappreciative becomes the unappreciated
The new sound becomes a song outdated
You became a hollow sound in an empty room.
Echoes fall on deaf ears
You're the only one who can hear your own pain
Yet you blame the walls
For holding you hostage inside
The one who's responsible for it all
Is the same person who won't swallow their pride.
I saw the disappointment in your eyes
But you know how to pretend
The loneliest person who's convinced himself that he
doesn't need a friend.
I let you deprive me
I let you convince me to give you another chance
The fastest route to a dead end
I was unappreciated by the unappreciative.
He took everything and I begged that you would give
Now that it is time for the tables to turn
And wounds are starting to burn
You're begging for a friend
Who understands how it feels to be unappreciated.

Lovinglovingloving

You taught
me
how
to
be
lovinglovingloving
in
the
midst
of
drowning,
drowning,
drowning.

Proud eagle in the sky

I know you're not able to witness my mood swings
The tantrums I throw when I am unhappy
And the way I over analyze things
There wasn't much room down here for angels
So I hope you're able to enjoy the protection that heaven brings
I may have went days without calling
Taking advantage of the time that I thought we all deserved
I am sorry
And my regret is the only dish that's being served
I loved you more than I could ever proclaim
You loved me loudly
And I was blinded by the shame
I never believed I deserved it
Which showed the disconnection with myself
And through the hard times
I wish my life came with a closing curtain
There were moments of enthusiasm
There were times of sadness
But I could never see it in your face
I decided to accept your love

At the worst time
I accepted everything you begged me to call mine
I know once you get to heaven's gate
You will read your blessings aloud
And they'll ask about me
And you'll reply saying,
"Throughout my life, she has made me very proud."

Freedom

All the days you were in captive
All the days you felt inactive
The day you gave in to the pattern of the "has been"
You may be tired now
You may be color blind
One day you'll be able to see the flying colors
And you won't try to hide your eyes
The screaming aches your brain
The worry breaks your spine
You wonder all day and night
Will freedom ever be called mine?
I can reassure you
Almost vow a promise
There will be a day where the chains will break
And your doubt will leave the premise
You'll run through the storm
And your scars won't leave a blemish
Once you choose life
And you become someone instead of anyone
You will gain more and then some
And you'll celebrate
Your newfound individual freedom.

Fear

You will look back at fear

And laugh

That all this time

You thought fear had everything you had.

You will look back at fear

And laugh

That all this time

Fear never even had a chance.

Stay

HURRY
UP
&
STOP.
STAY WHERE YOU ARE.
AND BE GRATEFUL
FOR
EVERYTHING.
HURRY
UP
&
STOP!

Joy

At night
When I am laying there
I smile.
Because of the other time
And the other time
And that one time
Where we laughed
And we joked
And I found joy
In the presence of you
And I am guaranteed
That joy will stay
As long as you will too.

Polaroid

Captivated by the pictures on the wall
The greatest view of a fantastic fall
As we hang up our greatest moments
I continuously go through the motions
Remembering there was a cure for the love potion
I was a fool for you
A class act
You remained in a stagnant place
But the flash always looks past that
We looked happy in our hidden shame
That only a smile can avoid
There is no honesty
In the ink of a polaroid.

Fire

Do not run through the fire.
Walk.
Sit.

Careful

Reluctant, I am
I have mastered the art of hesitance
Why would I destroy myself again?
In the name of soul binding, demanding negligence.

I may look twice
I may give myself time
I may reread the situation again
To carefully prove my instinct right.

Have you ever ignored your soul?
Broke it in half
Then listened to it cry?

It
He
She.

Your soul is very much of you
And very much of me.

The soul carries a mind full
The strength to carry two
But I only have me
And that's why I'm careful.

Every
Day
We
Get
Closer
And
Closer
To
The
Day
Where
We
Can
No
Longer
Pretend.

This too shall pass

And this.
And this.
And that.

Medusa

Deadly
How deadly
can a mistake be.
How dangerous
To believe that beauty will heal your cold
Stone
Soul.

Construct

Build
A
Place
Where
Even
The
Loneliest
Feeling
Cannot
Find
You.

Fly

You have the strength to fly
But you've convinced yourself that you can only crawl.

Silly

Ha,
How silly is it?
For us
To force ourselves.
To describe a love
That can only be felt.

Nostalgia

Dear nostalgia,
I've met someone new.

The beginning of a new life.

MASTERY

"The Key to Mastery is Simplicity.
Commit to a Monomaniacal Focus and Practice Only a
Few Things.
Build Your Life Around the Vital Few.
Distraction Dilutes Your Genius."

– Robin Sharma

Chaotic

You've heard
Phone calls
Familiar voices
Car horns
Disappointments
Accomplishments
New beginnings
Bad endings
Love songs
Heartaches
Build ups
And torn down
Ideas
And failures
Accidents
Shows
Movies
Plays
And Playlists
Redos
And rewinds

But when your SOUL screams
You pay it no mind.

Distraction kills.

Happy/peace

Should I master happiness?
Or
Should I master peace?
One requires effort
While the other one only requires you to breathe.

Control

I have gathered the strength to move past
The willingness to force sick things to last
I have seen the ending
And it has left me drained
Dry
Nothing in this life that I love should make me cry
Only in the hands of the inevitable
The indescribable
And the unpredictable
Should I ever
Allow chaos
To sit at my life's table.

I may lose my patience
I may lose my hope
I may walk away from my joy
And put my passion on hold
But it is my responsibility to construct a life
And become a person that's whole.

I can't control the outside
And I can barely grasp the inside

But to breathe again
And try to reach for a better life
That's where I'll be proud
That's where I will set my pride.

Divide and Conquer

Tackle that reckless
Doubtful
Hostile
Meaningless
Angry
Saddened
Part of yourself
And
BURY IT.
To
Live
Is
To
See
Yourself
Die
Over
And
Over
In
The
Midst

Of
Your
Troubling
Times.

                              Conquer Your Giants.

"I Digress"

You cannot drown your worries in the sea of regret
For the tide is high and your memories will surface
The vastness of water serves a higher purpose,
You use the depths for hiding
An action wrapped up in hopelessness
The waves are meant for cleansing
Yesterdays are meant for releasing
The longer you hold your breath underwater
The more your life is decreasing.

Worship the waves
Appreciate the sea
For it holds more regret
Than the lives of you and me
Let go of the patterns
Stop throwing your own stones
For it will be a waste of flesh
And a pity on your bones.

End Self Pity.

"Dynamic/Dynamite"

Explosive

Implosive

Souls of the **lost** and **abrasive**

Quietly kept and avoiding life lessons

Unaware of the danger they embrace in.

You, a flame.

Interact with this danger in the form of friends

You speak life into dead souls

And they

All

React

The

Same.

You, a flame.

Invite the explosive into your home

And the dangerous know you by your name

You speak your dreams instead of their patterns

And they

All

React

The

Same.

You, a flame.
Unintelligently ignite a spark
It only takes one time
For the EXPLOSIVE
IMPLOSIVE
MOUTHS
TO
RIP
YOUR
LIFE
APART.

Master the protection of your dreams.

"Prayer for Mastery"

Mastery
Master Me
Engulf my naivety
With your history.

I've heard of your discipline
And your prosperity
Influence my laziness
With a heart of gratefulness
For a grateful heart is a M A G N E T for miracles
At least that's what I heard.

Mastery
Master Me.
Prove to me
That you're more than just a word.

Master Truth

The truth is destructive
A mere sense of insanity
The smoke in the fire becomes clearer
All while the walls you put up
Suddenly decide to become mirrors.
You cover your eyes
Pretending to be blind
To all the darkness that you hide inside
Challenging your soul
Perceiving outsiders as your only "threat"
Oh darling
You haven't met yourself yet.
Master your own divinity
Your small sense of self
Is only a reflection of infinity.
There is only one limit
There is only one source of being
The deeper you dig into your cries
You find that there is no such thing.
The cries you hear are only a response
The darkness you see is only an absence
You, a never-ending conquest

Cannot dwell in that madness
Labeled as regret.
Truth is what you deny
Truth is who you refuse to be
Truth is the lowest version of you
And the highest version of me.
The truth comes out
Through and through
Truth destroys every facade
Until there's nothing left
But you.

Master light

"All colors depend on light."

All death depends on is more life
The catastrophe turns into a beautiful masterpiece
I deeply admired the light rays between you and me
Auras in the sky was nothing but a subtlety
I arrived at the right time.

I discovered that there was more to life than absence
But if this doesn't show up
There's more to life than its presence
The light
A chameleon
Can shine in the beauty of a thousand nights
And you limit yourself to such a small size.

Your light is not wrong
It doesn't take up too much space
Your light is always radiant
Shining in such an appropriate place.

You need the burning sensation
The eye watering, head cringing sight of a new foundation
You cannot have love, without me
Light is nothing but a mere sense of sanity
A reminder of endless possibility
Light, an endless sight.
You've been searching for love in the darkness
As your soul disguised itself as nothing
But the absence
Of
The
Night.

Master Night

Don't
Chase
The
Shadows
Of
The
Broken
Hearted
Allow
Yourself
To
Rebuild
Your
Kingdom
Again
And
Again.
Allow
The
Day
To
Remind

You
That
Darkness
Is
Also
A
Close
Friend.

Master Grace

Every breath
Undeserved.
Every
Single
One
But
You
Still
Continue
To
Thrive
Because
God
Believes
You
Still
Deserve
The
Time.

Master Day

You continue to inspire me
You
A sight after darkness is done
You
A safe haven for the mightiest of suns
You are the clouds in the sky
The song that birds sing
You have the right amount of gratefulness
For the forgiveness that a new day brings
I belong to you.

I fell asleep to my worries
Badgered at my time
When the light hit my eyelids
I realized that all time could be mine

You have been the most reliable source of light
You have been the backbone of countless centuries
You are the reason we each have fallen
You are the reason we all have tasted our pride.

You remind me how to be mindful
In
A
Life

That's
Obsessed
With
Having
A
Mind
Full.

Master Kindness

You've held hands with the supernatural
The all powerful
The disastrous
And the unrelenting
Yet, you still notice me as an entire being
When I only see a sight not worth seeing
You follow me home, just in case I decide to switch paths
You were always asking me why I never enjoyed class-
I felt undervalued
Unappreciated
And overseen
You saw me with no intention
You saw me when there was an alternative decision
You made me your priority
And I was against self-discovery
It never made sense
That someone can love me more than I could love myself.

I saw a monster
You saw a goddess
You wanted my beauty to shine throughout the atmosphere
And I wanted to remain modest.

The last time I saw you I decided to embrace the part of
myself
That I begged God to leave on the bottom shelf
You convinced me that the only part of me that is worth
focusing on is my mind
You've convinced me that the only person alive is me
And I'm the only one that's worthy enough of wasting my
time
You've helped me move my own man-made mountains
And you've celebrated my life in the midst of my cry
All the resistance I've put between you and I
And you never forgot
To be kind.

Master Strength

One rainy day, I was at the hospital with my late
grandfather.
We both were waiting on him to receive a treatment that
required body fluid being drawn.
In order to draw the blood, the nurse would have to use a
needle the size of a computer screen, and I was terrified
for him. While waiting, I noticed a young child sitting next
to his mother across the room. I was dumbfounded,
wondering why such a young child was here waiting in the
same treatment room. His mother and my grandfather
started talking, and we found out that her child was here
for the same treatment as my grandfather. Surprisingly, he
went first. When he came back to the room, he was just as
calm as he was when he left.
And I may not know what disease he was battling with,
I may not know his name,
I may not know his age,
I may not know if he even had won,
But I am certain of this
This young boy had found his strength
And while I was sitting there
Panicking

Worrisome
And unsure of what lay ahead
That young boy showed me that in the face of pain and
adversity
That your soul could be so calm
You could loudly drop a pen.

Master Wrong

YOU ARE DEAD WRONG ABOUT
EVERYTHING
YOU ARE DEAD WRONG ABOUT EVERYONE
YOU ARE DEAD WRONG ABOUT WHO YOU ARE
AND SINCE YOU'RE ALWAYS WRONG

You might as well have some fun.

Master Right

You listen to the outpouring feeling of exhaustion
That's the sound of your righteous soul.

EARTH

EUPHORIA

"Huge difference between being happy at will
And chasing euphoric moments as an escape.
One doesn't cost a dime,
the other
will
tax
your
soul."
– T.F Hodge

Lair

You're my hiding place
A corner of a room, dimly lit
Often overlooked by those who want to be in the sunshine
I look for you in the dark
I retreat to you,
when I want to be free.

Oscillation

Describe our love in one word: motion.

Two bodies

One Experience

Moving constantly

In a forward, demanding direction

I believed it was time for us to leave

I grabbed your hand and you reminded me not to leave

myself behind

I should've checked the time

We've been stuck in the past

Because we refuse to let the present doubt ruin what's

mine——

I mean ours.

We've spent hours waiting on our first fight

I have a peace of mind

Once I gave you a piece of my

Undeserving

Self-absorbed

Lonely nature

I've come to deserve

Out of all the hearts I have

You're the only heart that I'll preserve

I've been in love before
At least that's what I've believed
The gravitation that our lost souls have
Hint an unfamiliar scheme
The gentle feeling of summer that gleams across your
smile as you wait for me to come home
I hear your name in all the love songs
Even the ones that result in broken bones
Disappointment found in a broken soul
Because I know once it's time for you to go
Sorrow will be the only song I'll know
I've been in love before
At least that's what I believed was mine
Until I met you.
I realized I was alone the whole time.

There probably
won't be
another chance
to tell you
about how
I felt the
first time
but I'll
make sure
I'll never
have to
tell you
for the
last time.

In love with the idea of being in love.

Unrequited

The stars aligned on time
For the first time I believed that was mine
I heard that loving yourself was the type of love to get lost
in
But I enjoyed the aroma and disgust of your sin
I envied you
I was jealous of your carelessness in a world full of
consequences
I felt like they only sought after me
But how could this be?
The touch that we both feel
The kiss as mysterious as the bottom of the sea
I called you just to hear your voice
And I didn't want to do it
But I felt like I didn't have a choice
You were running from your repercussions
And I was engrossed in your discussion
I didn't want to be disappointed in myself
And you never wanted to be true

I was ashamed to be me
But I was ecstatic to be with you.

Don't confuse pain with passion.

Thunder

A thunderstorm
Your heart makes
When the lightning strikes
And your pride breaks
Apart and apart
It shatters like glass
The roar of the doubtful shakes
As your happiness flies past
The rain water cleanses you
As you release the fears
The pent-up anger results
In the most beautiful of tears
A thunderstorm
Your heart makes
When the lightning strikes
And your pride breaks
A sunny day
Your life creates
When you let the thunderstorm pass
And don't send it away.

Quarantine

HEALTHY!
How HEALTHY!
Is the smile on your face when you saw me!
Peace came along for the ride
I walked to your bed
And your body was diseased
I can tell that your medicine
Was the joy that you refused to breathe
I saw you
Laying there
Unaware of your physical power
And disappointed in your mental cower
I carried your passion when you didn't see it
I held your faith when you didn't believe it
I fed you when you didn't have the strength to eat
I held your heart together when your tendons wouldn't
meet
You wanted to stay in the same cycle
And I demanded that you release yourself from the rinse
and repeat
I did what was needed to make you live again
And you sustained a new life and became your own friend

HEALTHY!
How HEALTHY!
Is the smile on your face when you saw me!
And when it was time for me to leave
I left you
Healthy.

Home

In my house of gratitude we will serve love
In my house of serenity we will serve hope
In my house of sovereignty we will serve love.
In my house, we belong here.
And in my house, I belong here.

Truth

All we do is lie
Lie to each other about our well-being
We fight against our wits
We move onto other people
Piling up the souls in our soul's bottomless pit
I should applaud you
For the reasoning, so it seems
That every time you opened your heart up
You were ashamed of what truth it brings
I hope you know that heaven sings
Whenever you open your eyes
And that God laughs
At your petty little mistakes
Your ancestors wonder why you're so hard on yourself
While your reflection sees a hero that's only missing a
cape
One day the truth will catch up to you
With nothing to say
But a million things to show
The truth will show you how high above ground you are
When you convince yourself that you're mighty below
The truth will sing a song of power

A song of courage
A song of resilience
The song that your soul cried out everyday
Yet it was the type that you deemed irrelevant
The truth waited to show you something special
And you focused on the detrimental
You saw your life as something less than
And the truth saw it as plentiful
All we do is lie
Convince ourselves that the truth is opposite of the light
One day you'll find your lies couldn't dim your darkness
The way your darkness is dimmed by your light.

Tomorrow

How
Wonderful
Of
A
Feeling
Is
It
To
Know
That
The
Same
Souls
That
Love
You
Today
Will
Always
Love
You
Tomorrow.

Dream catcher

In a world
Obsessed with reality
You demand that I defy gravity
In a world
That's centered around poverty
You remind me that I am not only rich
But that I also live a life that is wealthy
In a world
Where letting go is difficult
You allow life to run its course
In t
he face of a life that's so sinful
In a world
Where the ending is near
You laugh in the face of adversity
And ask the bartender for another beer
In a world
Obsessed with reality
As awful as it seems
You're the only part of my reality,
that demands that I dream.

Blinded

All the love that surrounds you
Isn't always romantic
The love you live
Isn't always platonic
There's love in the air you breathe.
The food that you eat
Behind every single act
Is someone behind it wanting it to be great
Not only for them
But for you
And everyone else
Who is in their rear view
Love consumes
Love transforms
Love hears you out
And love doesn't conform
Life is always headlining
Even when you can't see it perform
You are always surrounded by love
Even when you can't feel its warmth.

Maybe

Maybe
Just maybe
For you there will always be a maybe
The only one who can never receive a no
The only reason I don't want to give you a yes
Because I'm nervous that my yes may not be my personal
best
So instead of no
I'll say maybe so
Maybe it's true that there's a life without you,
Maybe it's true that there could be a day without your sly,
coveted smile
Maybe it's true that only suffering will only last a while
Maybe for you
Maybe is the only answer that you deserve
On a day that you can't stop berating me with accusations
that get on my last nerve
Maybe for you
I'll change the direction of my intention
Maybe for you
I'll believe in what's between us than what's around us
Maybe for you

I'll hold onto the rose full of thorns knowing how awful it
stings
Maybe for you
I'll still sink to the bottom of the ocean knowing there is
no way for me to breathe
Maybe for you
I'll consider you by yourself and value the person you are
when you're with me
If a maybe can give me this euphoric feeling of living in a
fantasy
Maybe for you
And there will always be
A Maybe
For me…

Peaceful / piece of something full

Peaceful
Peaceful
Is peace really full?

Can you pour out your peace?
Is it overflowing?
Can you talk to your peace
And find it never to be boring?

Is peace a part of you
Or is it your being?
Do you yourself end
When your peace is only beginning?

I believe that you see yourself as an incomplete
Lack of being
You dread being only partly whole
While your soul's passion is singing

In this life
You have to have a foundation
And the part of you that is peace
Is only a part of your stimulation.

There's more to you than you think.

Rebirth / Release

Hands quivering
Red and sore
Bones breaking and bending
As my brain convinced my hand that it wants more
Blood rushing
As the rope gets tighter and tighter
The screaming of my insecurity heightens
As the sight of the destruction gets brighter and brighter.
The tiresome feeling
Of almost losing a limb
Could not compare to the thought
Of living a life without them, him, her, us
The strike from the betrayal hit me below my bust
I had to release
Set my soul on ease
The restriction from catastrophic world
Didn't let the heart of my freedom breathe.

Release
Rebirth
Rehearse
Redo

Free yourself from the bonds
For the bonds will never release themselves from you.

Let Go / Cut Ties.

How happy is time
Endless in its essence
Bountiful in its entirety
Joyful in the destruction
And
In
The
Rebirth
Of
You
And
Me.

You have the right to move on.

Epilogue

I am
A
Human
Who
Is
Obsessed
With
Chasing
Humanness
Every
Flesh
Devouring
Spine
Tingling
Moment
That
Reassures
Us
Of
Our
Mortality.
Bury

Your
Light
Near
The
Truth.

Kharis A. Reedus is a dreamer. After releasing her first book, *Lost: A Release of Bondage from an Overly Xommitted Soul*, she has become dedicated to creating art that tells the truth about her experiences. Outside of writing, Kharis can be found obsessing over film, music, and art. She resides in the Bay Area, with her mother and little brother. She will conquer the world.

www.ingramcontent.com/pod-product-compliance
Lightning Source LLC
Chambersburg PA
CBHW061503050726
47593CB00002B/435